THE PHILLIP KEVEREN SERIES · EASY PIANO

GEORGE GERSHWIN CLASSICS

— PIANO LEVEL —
EARLY INTERMEDIATE

ISBN 978-1-4768-7544-6

World headquarters, contact:
Hal Leonard
7777 West Bluemound Road
Milwaukee, WI 53213
Email: info@halleonard.com

In Europe, contact:
Hal Leonard Europe Limited
42 Wigmore Street
Marylebone, London, W1U 2RN
Email: info@halleonardeurope.com

In Australia, contact:
Hal Leonard Australia Pty. Ltd.
4 Lentara Court
Cheltenham, Victoria, 3192 Australia
Email: info@halleonard.com.au

PREFACE

George and Ira Gershwin helped define the musical template of the Jazz Age. From 1924 until George's death in 1937, the brothers crafted over two dozen scores for Broadway and Hollywood. The songs that emerged from this period became the backbone of the Great American Songbook.

This collection is arranged to be playable by the developing pianist. My goal was to keep as much of the innate sophistication of these musical gems intact as possible, while making them technically accessible. In the process of writing these arrangements, I became an even bigger Gershwin fan than I was at the outset of the project. These songs were built to last!

Great tunes. Sublime lyrics. Together – magic. Who could ask for anything more?

Sincerely,

BIOGRAPHY

Phillip Keveren, a multi-talented keyboard artist and composer, has composed original works in a variety of genres from piano solo to symphonic orchestra. Mr. Keveren gives frequent concerts and workshops for teachers and their students in the United States, Canada, Europe, and Asia. Mr. Keveren holds a B.M. in composition from California State University Northridge and a M.M. in composition from the University of Southern California.

CONTENTS

BUT NOT FOR ME

from GIRL CRAZY

Music and Lyrics by GEORGE GERSHWIN
and IRA GERSHWIN
Arranged by Phillip Keveren

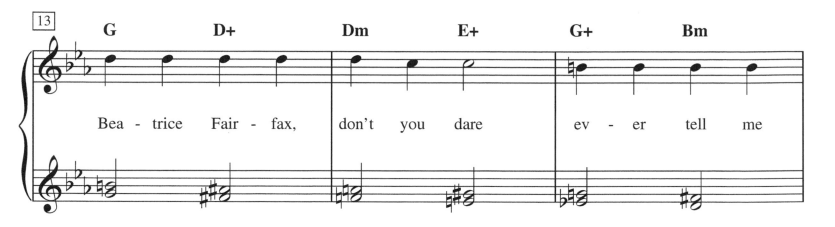

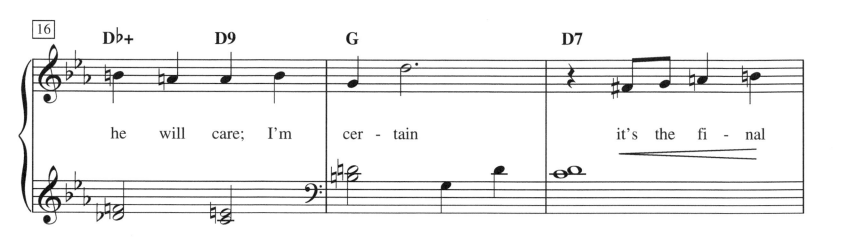

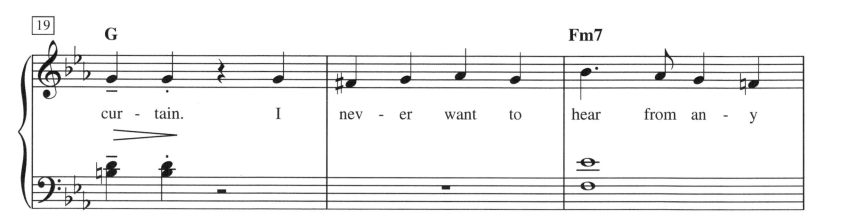

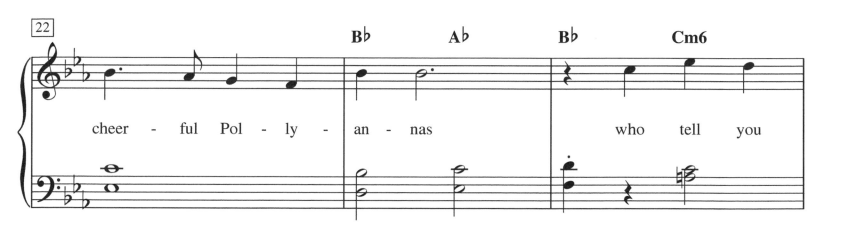

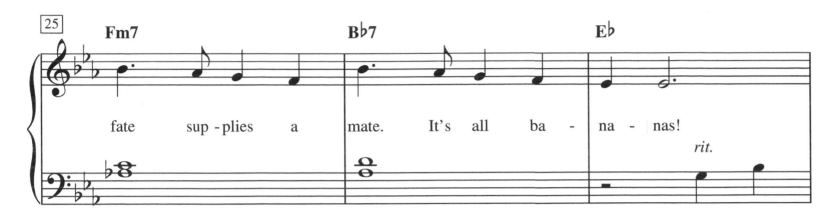

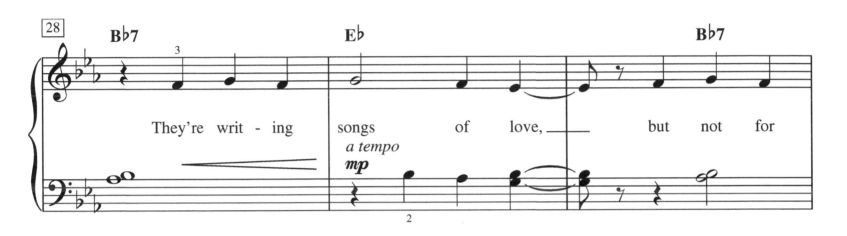

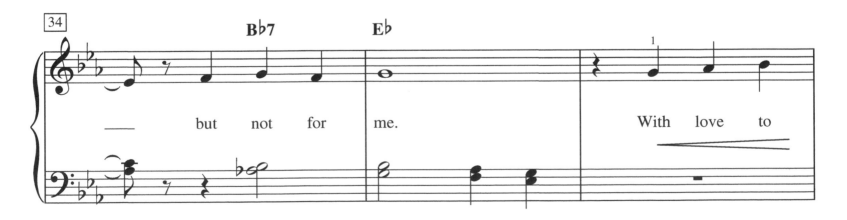

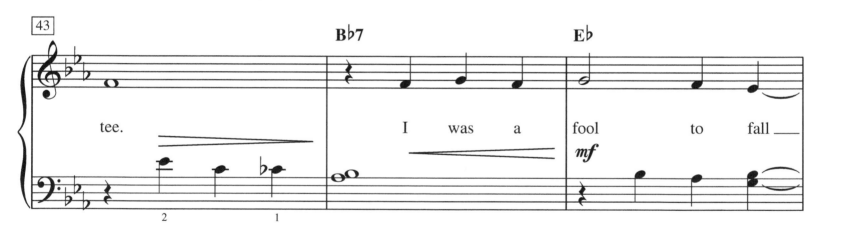

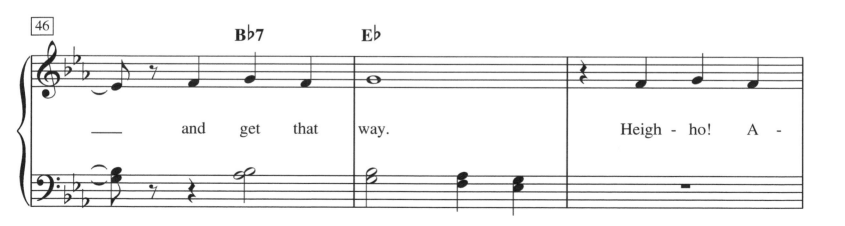

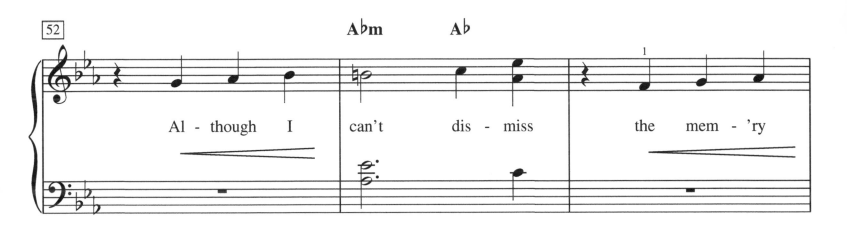

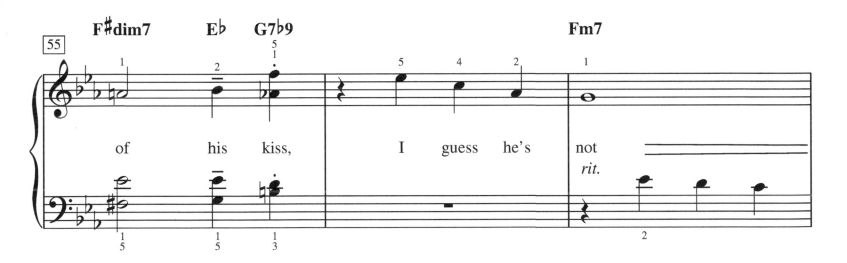

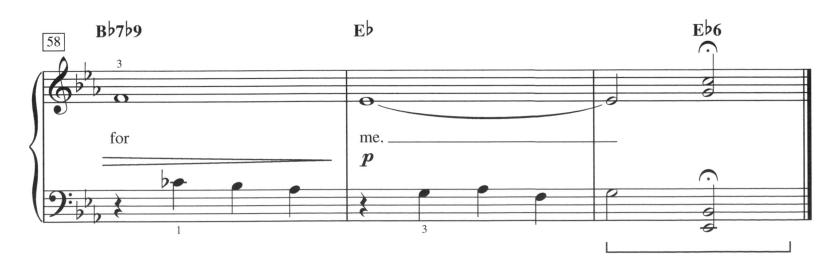

BY STRAUSS
from THE SHOW IS ON

Music and Lyrics by GEORGE GERSHWIN
and IRA GERSHWIN
Arranged by Phillip Keveren

Viennese Waltz ($\bullet$ = 160)

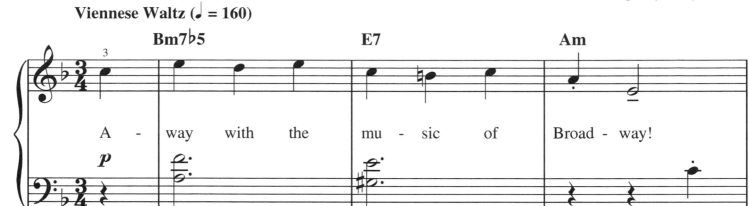

A - way with the mu - sic of Broad - way!

Be off with your Irv - ing Ber - lin!

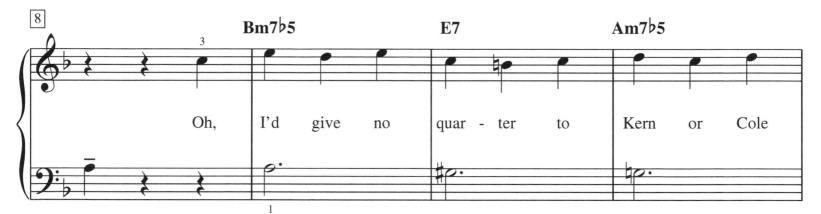

Oh, I'd give no quar - ter to Kern or Cole

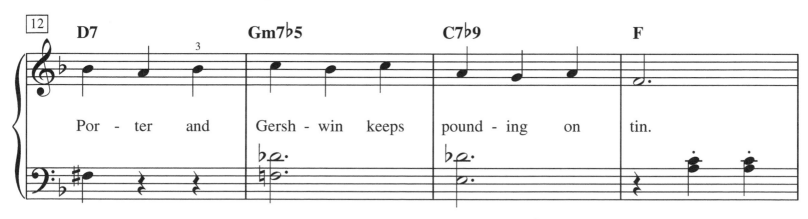

Por - ter and Gersh - win keeps pound - ing on tin.

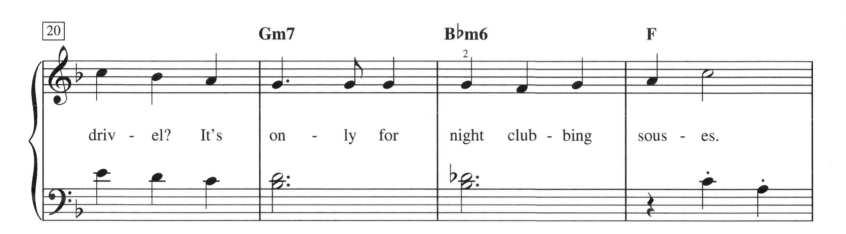

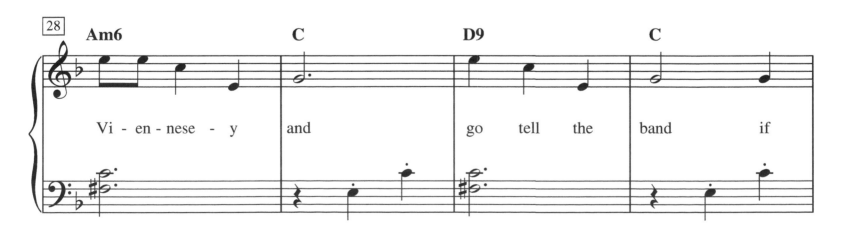

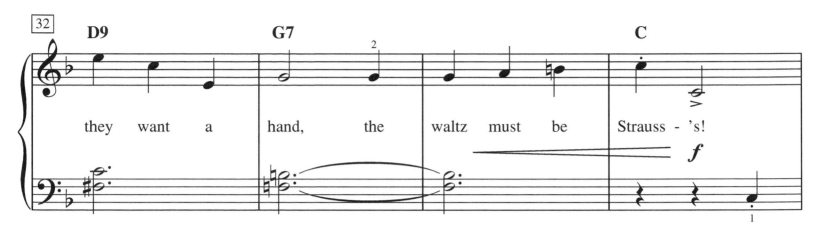

they want a hand, the waltz must be Strauss - 's!

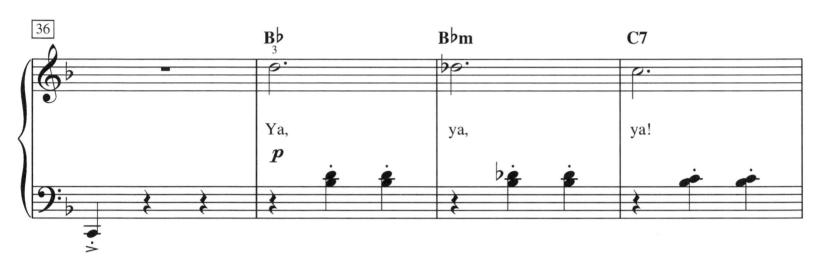

Ya, ya, ya!

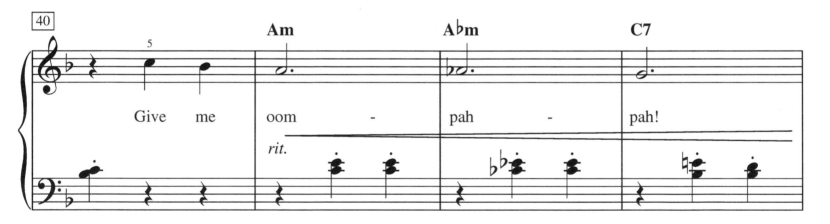

Give me oom - pah - pah!

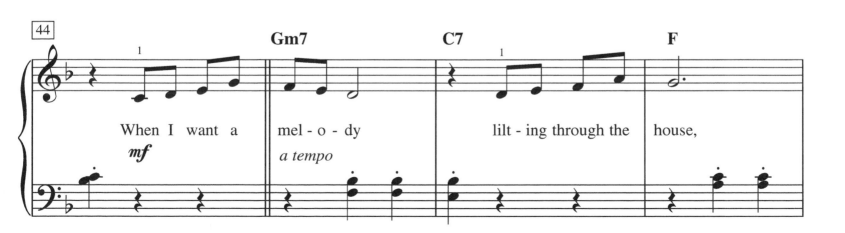

When I want a mel-o-dy lilt-ing through the house,

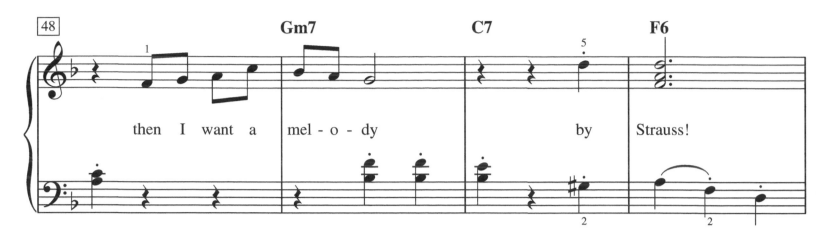

then I want a mel - o - dy   by   Strauss!

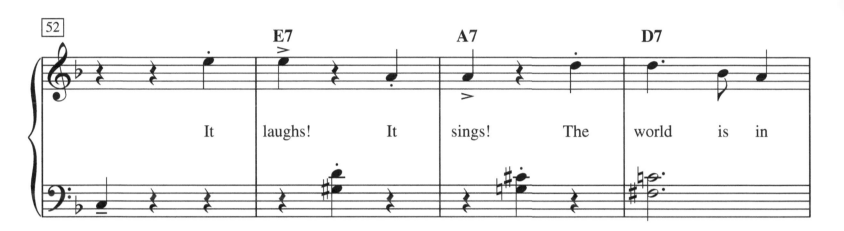

It   laughs!   It   sings!   The   world   is   in

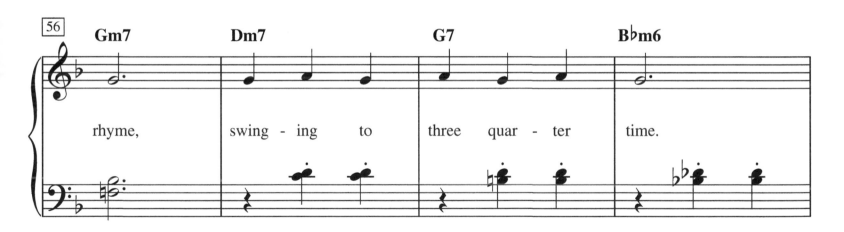

rhyme,   swing - ing   to   three   quar - ter   time.

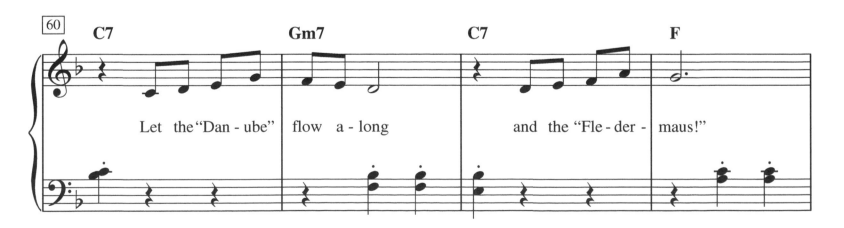

Let the "Dan - ube"   flow a - long   and the "Fle - der - maus!"

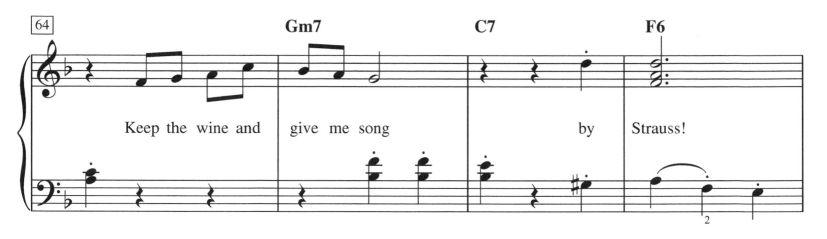

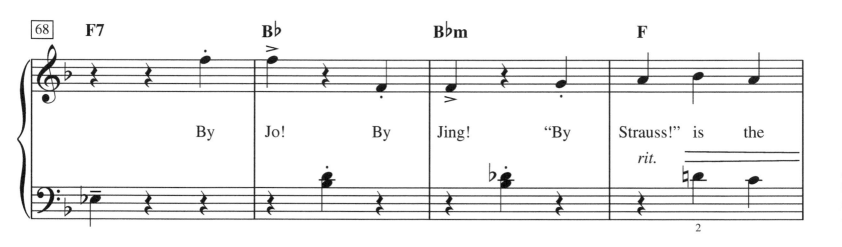

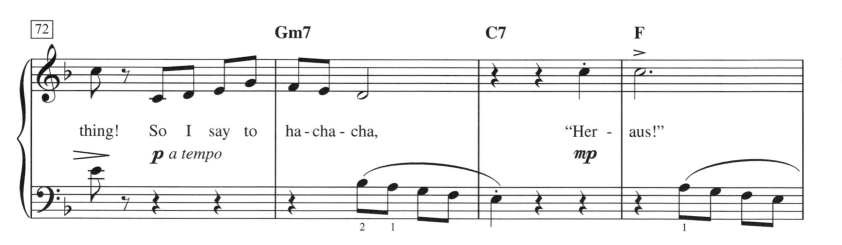

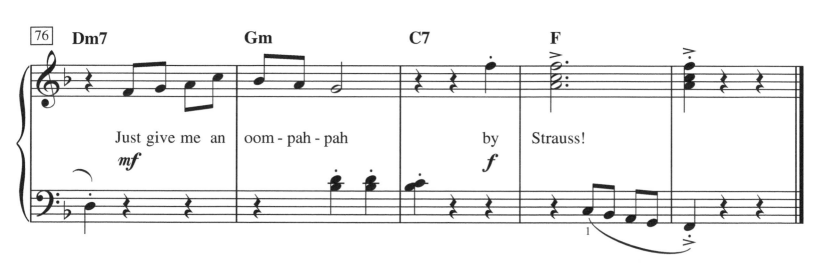

EMBRACEABLE YOU
from CRAZY FOR YOU

Music and Lyrics by GEORGE GERSHWIN
and IRA GERSHWIN
Arranged by Phillip Keveren

My in-tu-i-tion told me you'd come on the scene. La-dy,

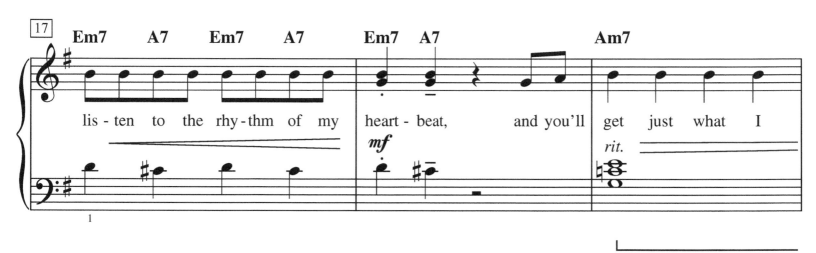

lis-ten to the rhy-thm of my heart-beat, and you'll get just what I

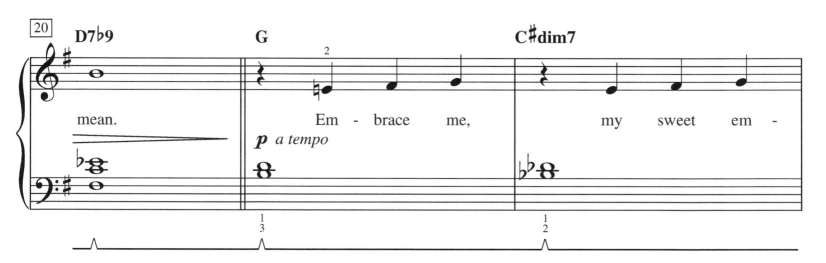

mean. Em-brace me, my sweet em-

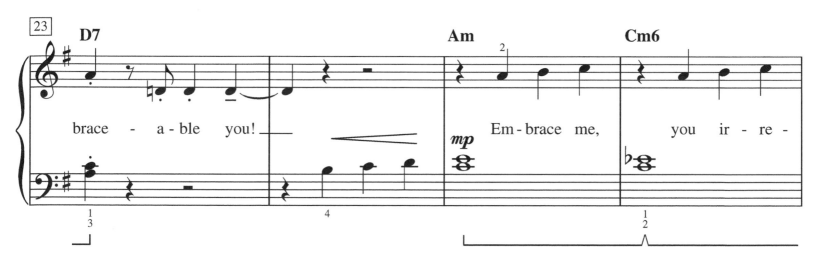

brace-a-ble you! Em-brace me, you ir-re-

16

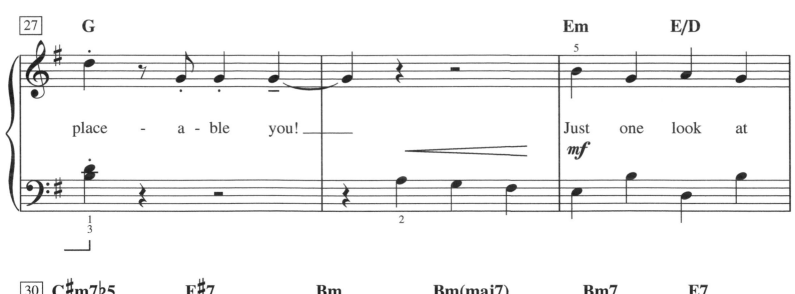

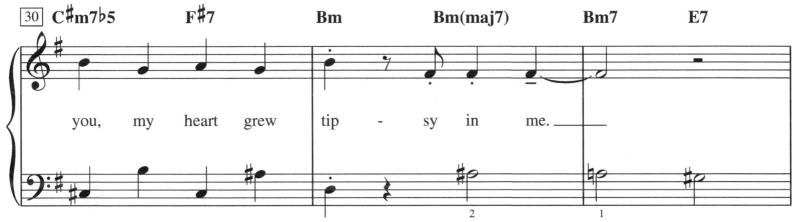

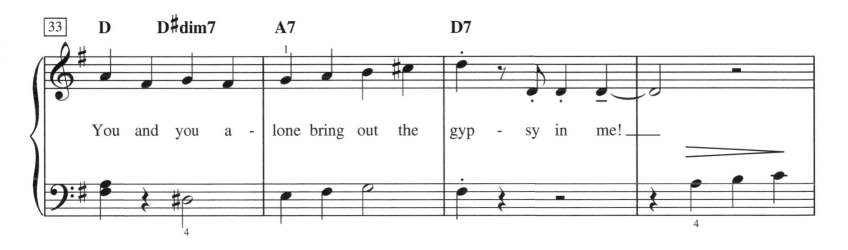

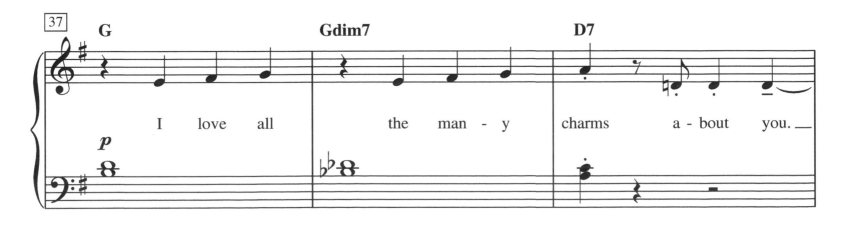

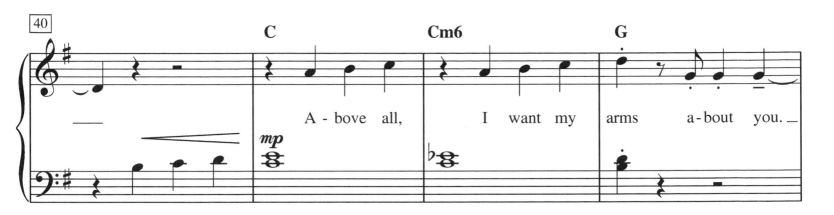

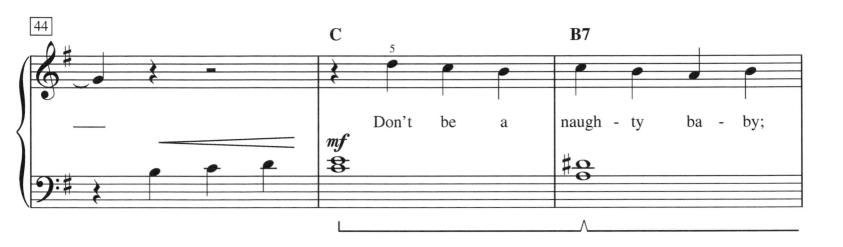

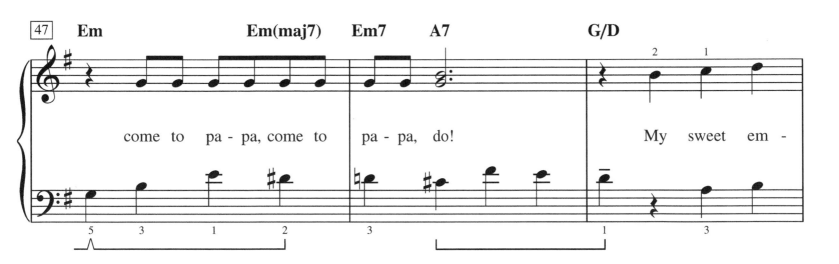

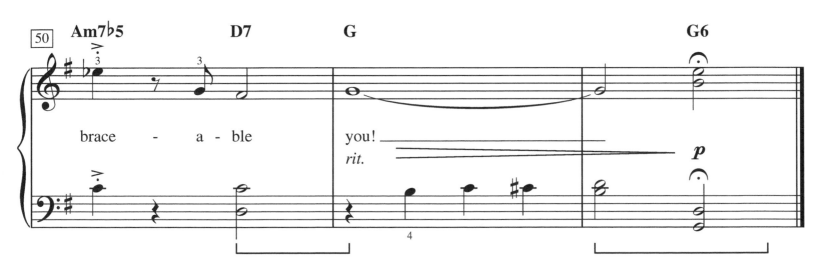

FASCINATING RHYTHM

from RHAPSODY IN BLUE

Music and Lyrics by GEORGE GERSHWIN
and IRA GERSHWIN
Arranged by Phillip Keveren

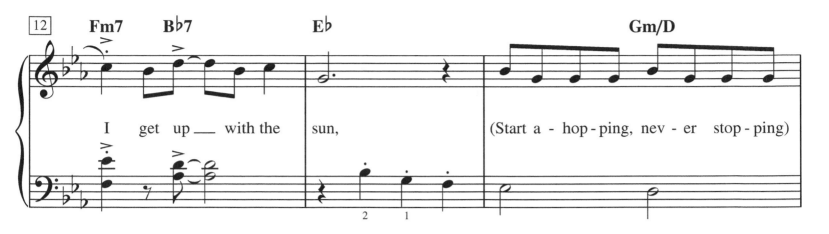

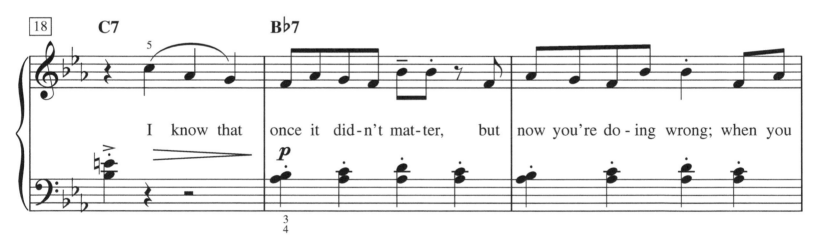

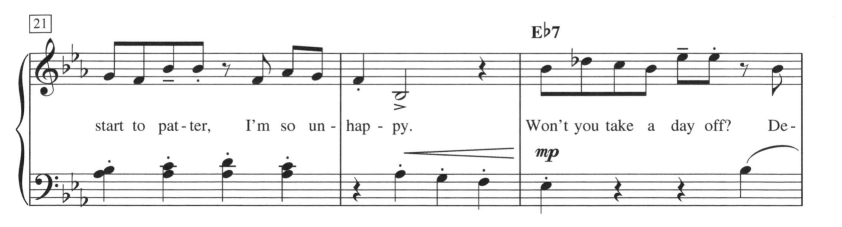

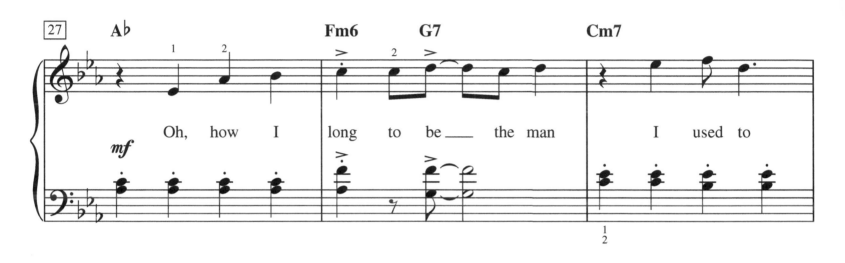

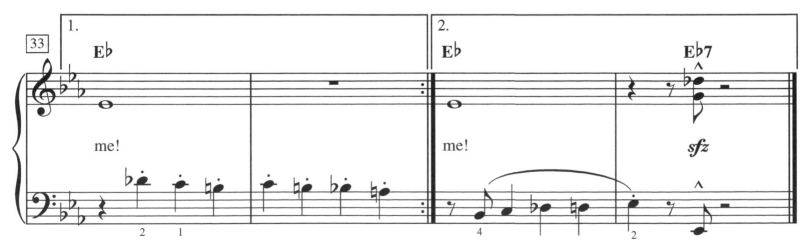

A FOGGY DAY
(In London Town)
from A DAMSEL IN DISTRESS

Music and Lyrics by GEORGE GERSHWIN
and IRA GERSHWIN
Arranged by Phillip Keveren

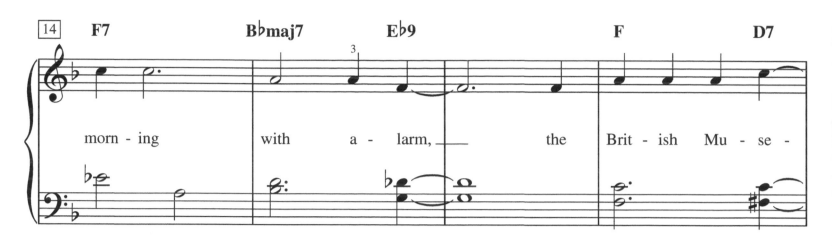

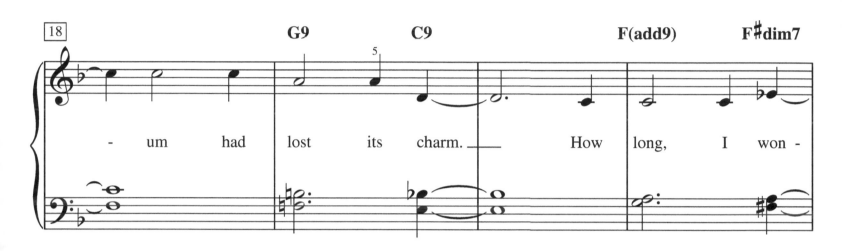

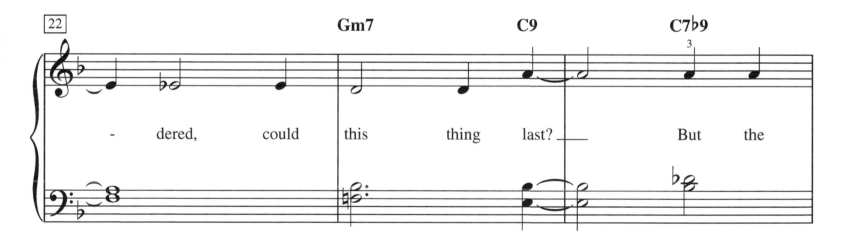

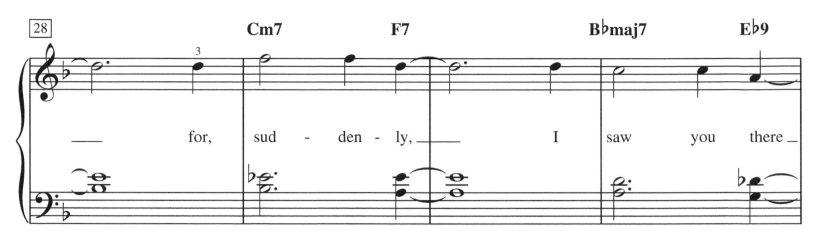

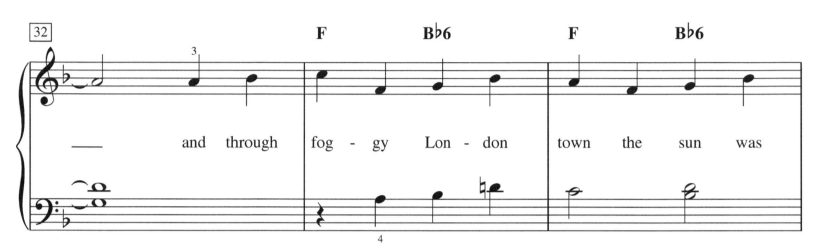

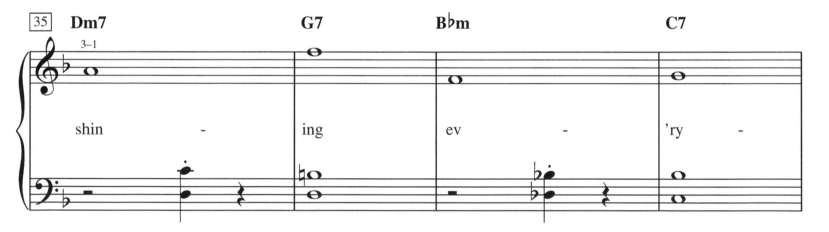

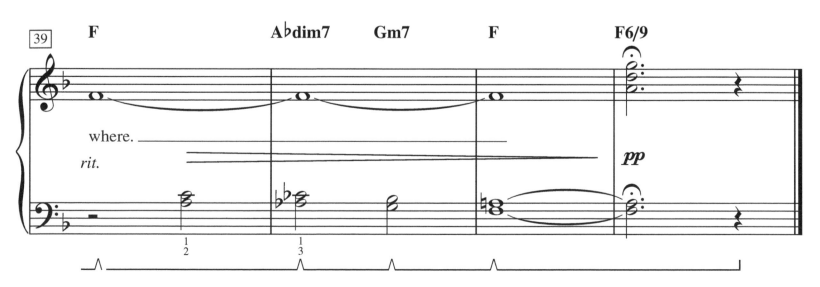

HOW LONG HAS THIS BEEN GOING ON?

Music and Lyrics by GEORGE GERSHWIN
and IRA GERSHWIN
Arranged by Phillip Keveren

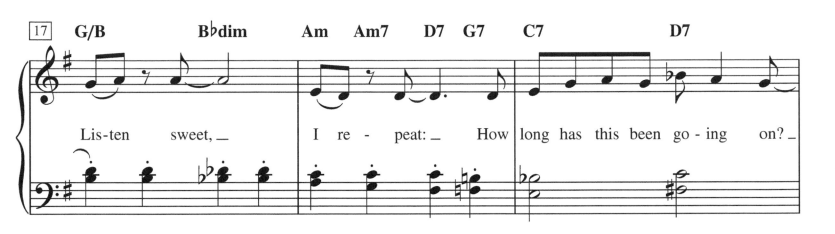

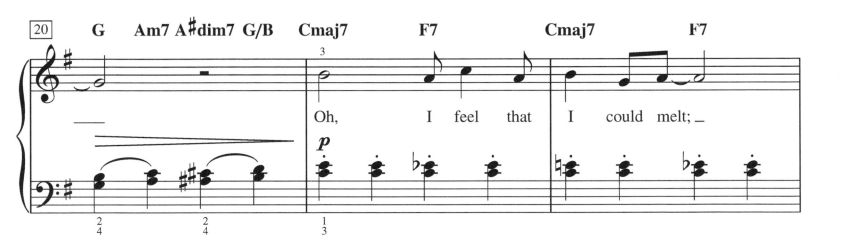

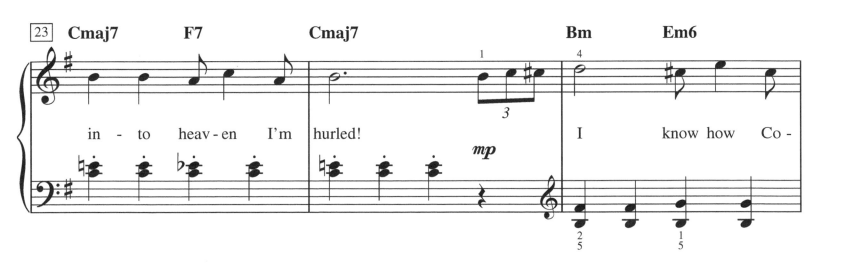

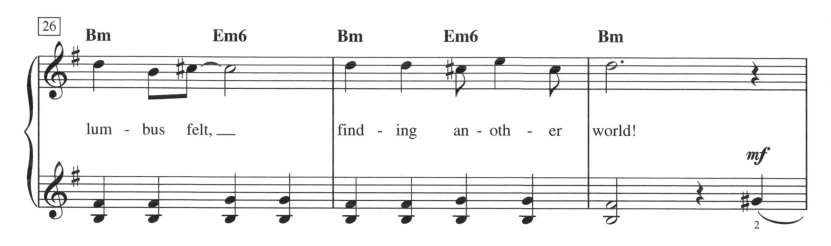

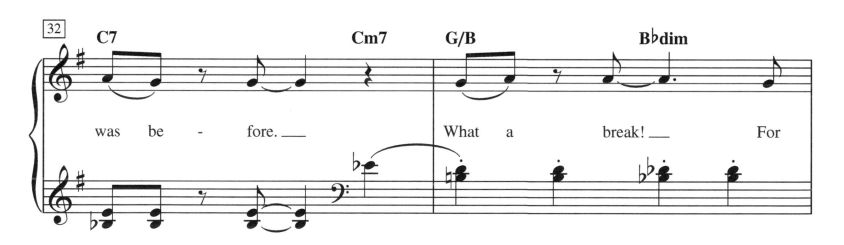

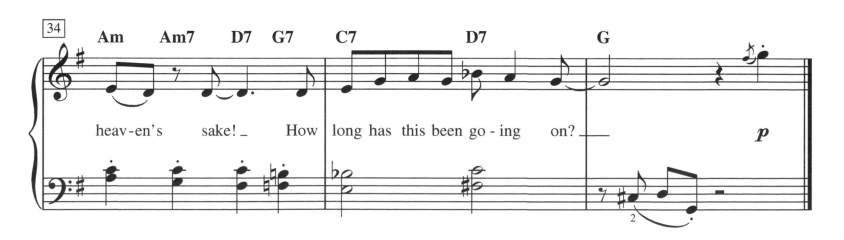

I GOT RHYTHM

from AN AMERICAN IN PARIS
from GIRL CRAZY

Music and Lyrics by GEORGE GERSHWIN
and IRA GERSHWIN
Arranged by Phillip Keveren

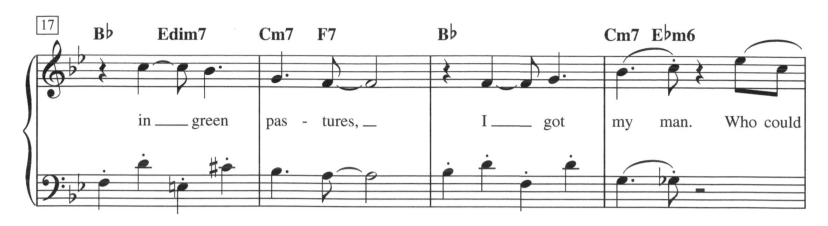

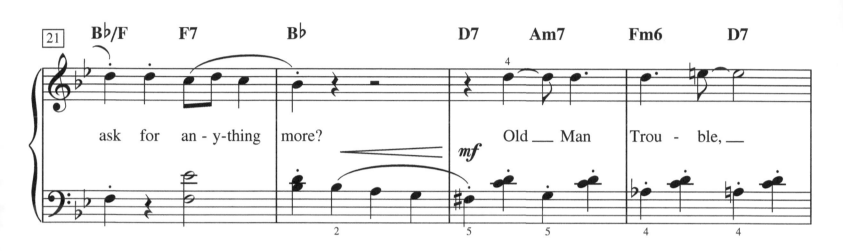

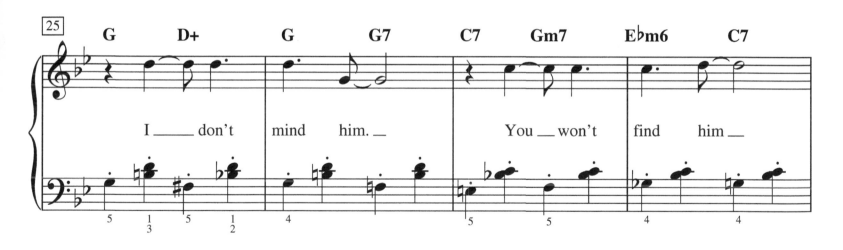

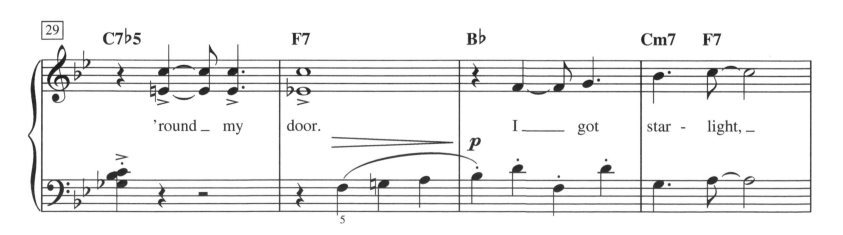

I ___ got sweet dreams, ___ I ___ got my man. Who could

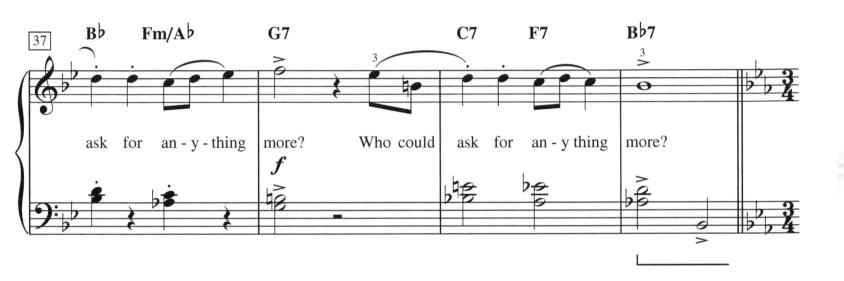

ask for an-y-thing more? Who could ask for an-y thing more?

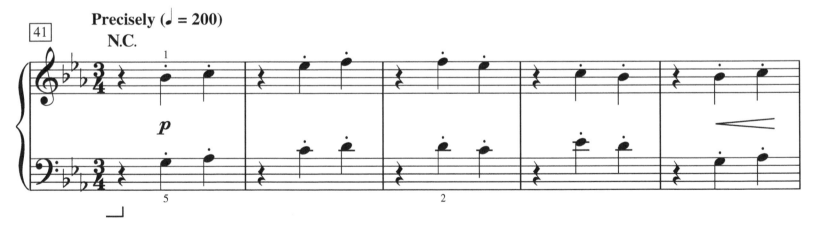

Precisely (♩ = 200)
N.C.

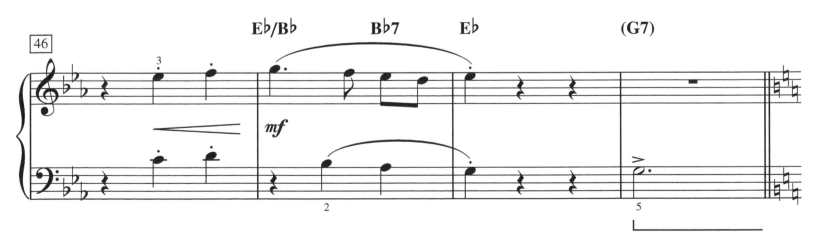

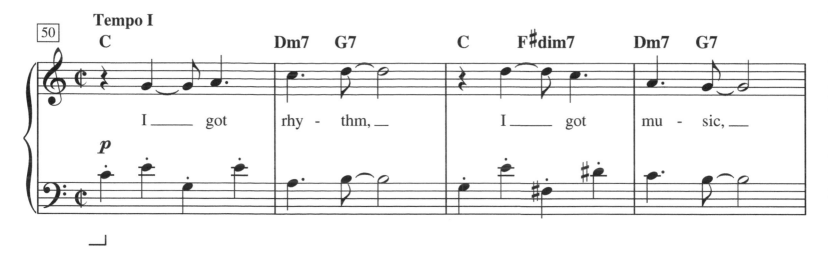

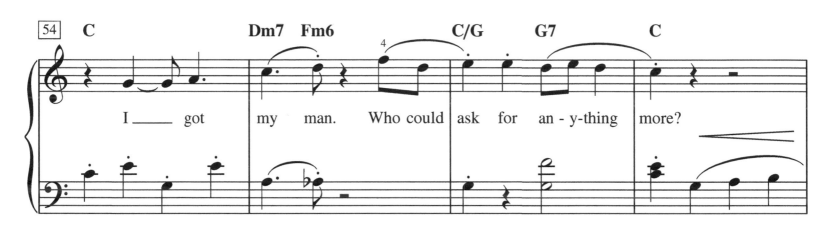

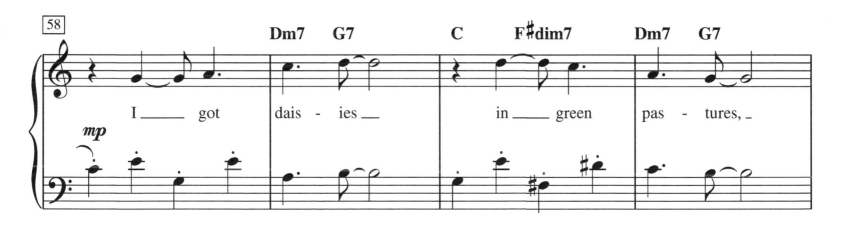

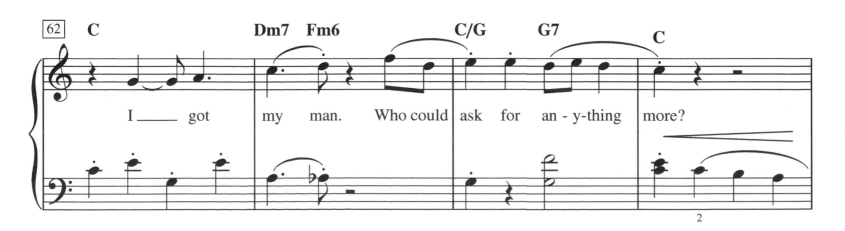

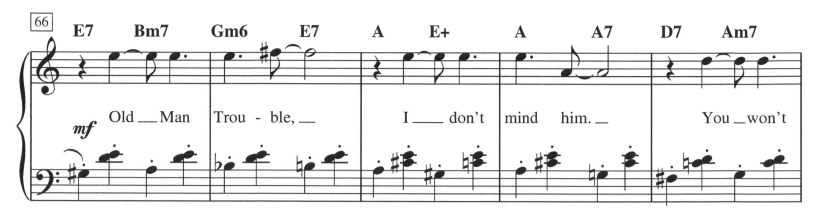

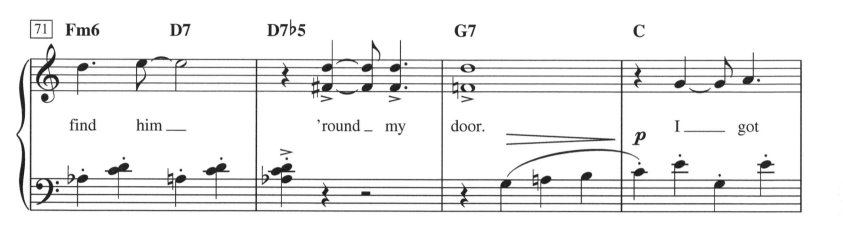

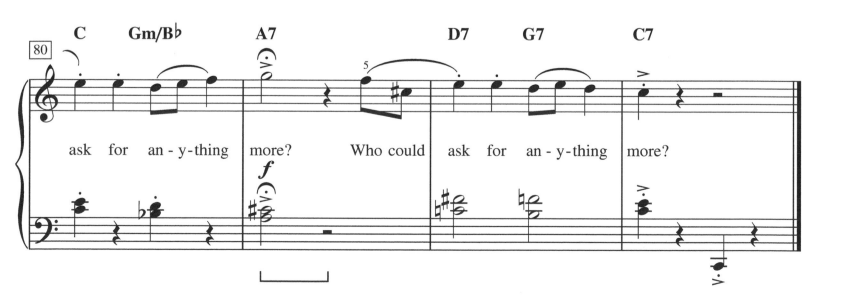

I'VE GOT A CRUSH ON YOU

from STRIKE UP THE BAND

Music and Lyrics by GEORGE GERSHWIN
and IRA GERSHWIN
Arranged by Phillip Keveren

Tenderly (♩ = 72)

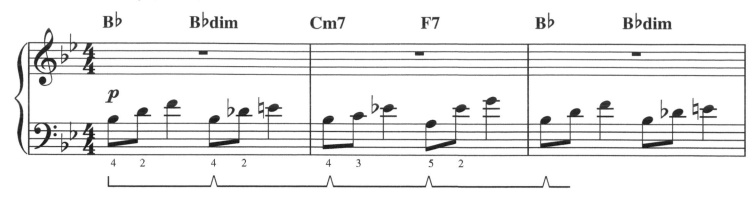

I've got a crush on you, — Sweet-ie Pie.

All the day and night-time hear me sigh. I nev - er had the least

no - tion — that I would fall with — so much e - mo - tion.

LOVE IS HERE TO STAY

from GOLDWYN FOLLIES
from AN AMERICAN IN PARIS

Music and Lyrics by GEORGE GERSHWIN
and IRA GERSHWIN
Arranged by Phillip Keveren

Freely expressive (♩ = 56-60)

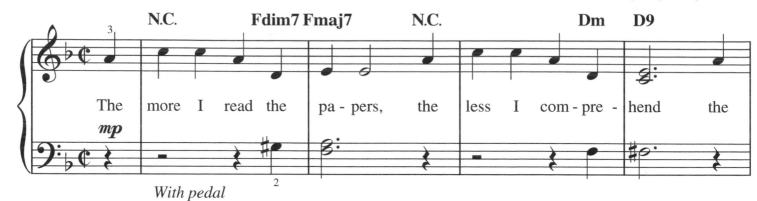

The more I read the pa-pers, the less I com-pre-hend the

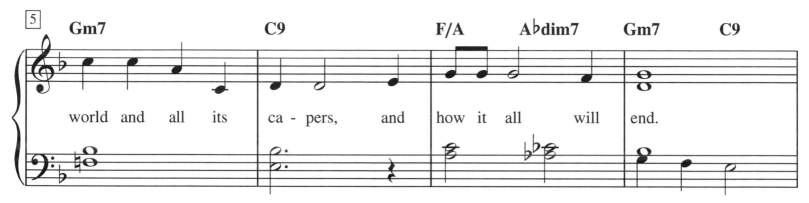

world and all its ca-pers, and how it all will end.

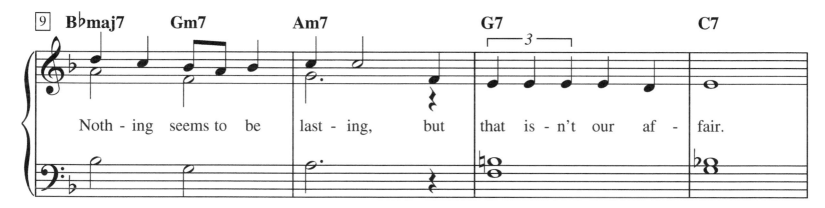

Noth-ing seems to be last-ing, but that is-n't our af-fair.

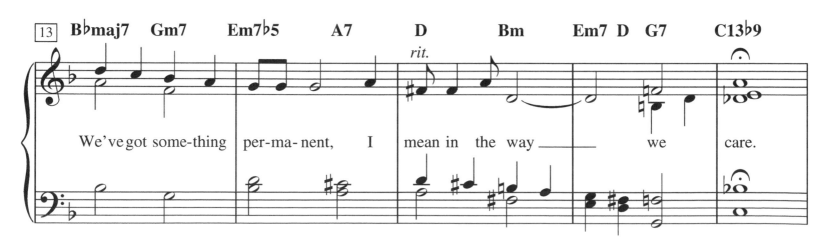

We've got some-thing per-ma-nent, I mean in the way we care.

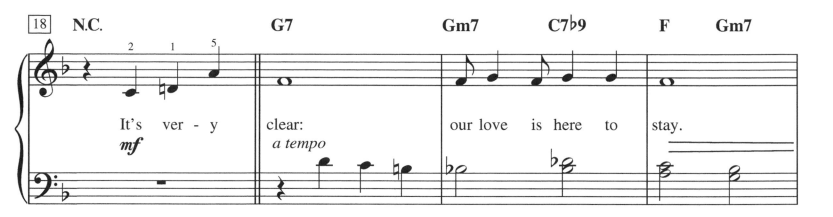

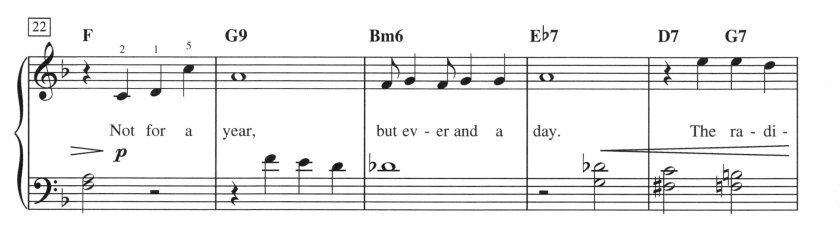

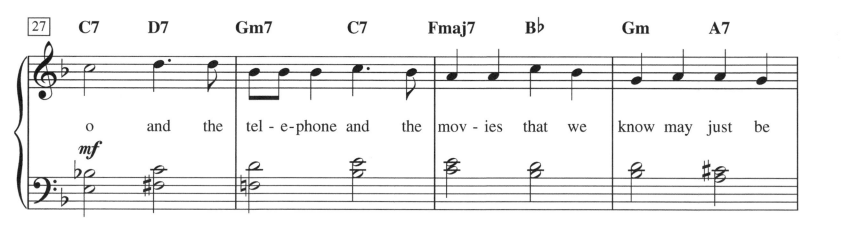

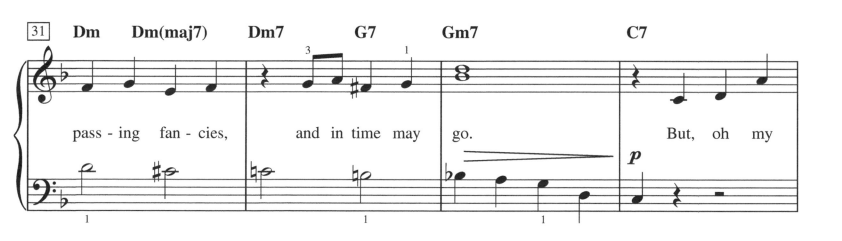

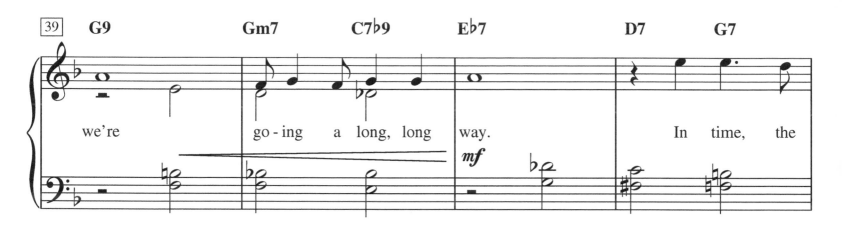

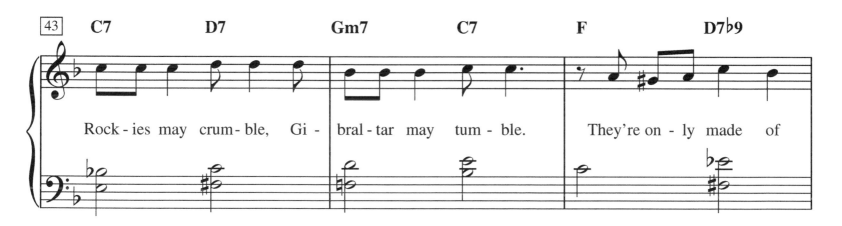

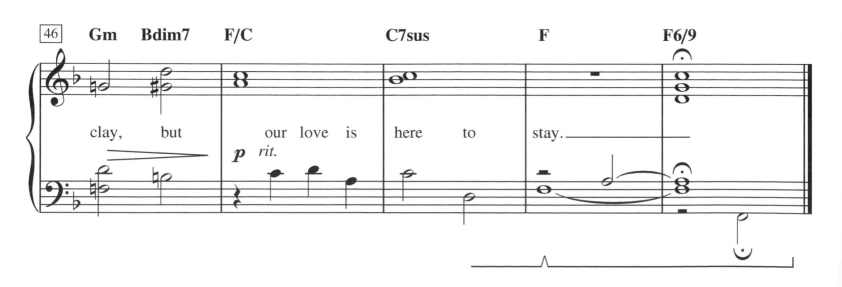

THE MAN I LOVE

from LADY BE GOOD
from STRIKE UP THE BAND

Music and Lyrics by GEORGE GERSHWIN
and IRA GERSHWIN
Arranged by Phillip Keveren

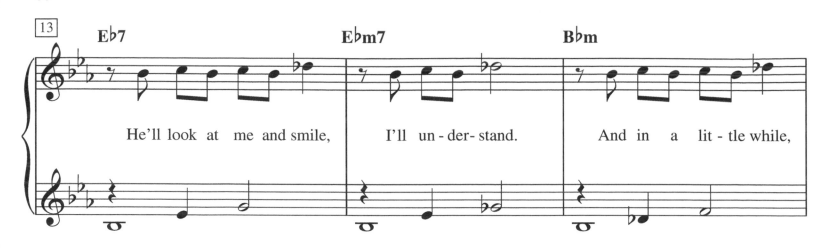

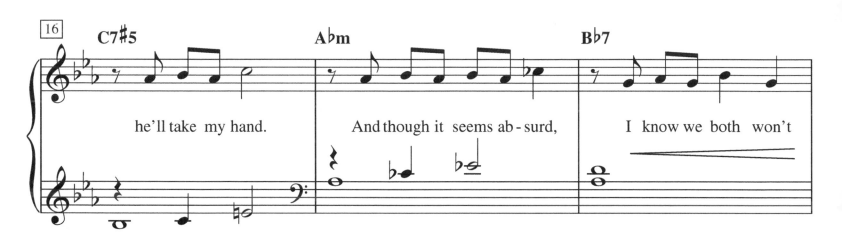

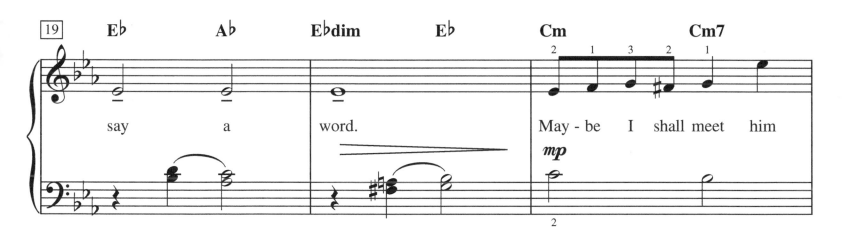

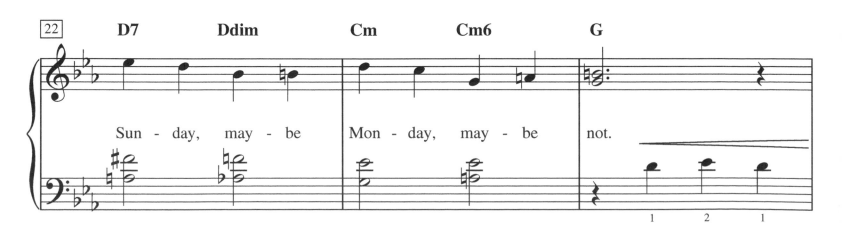

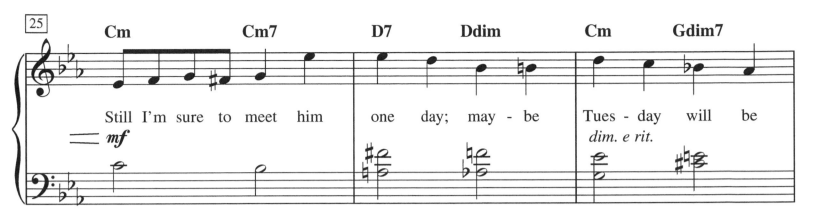

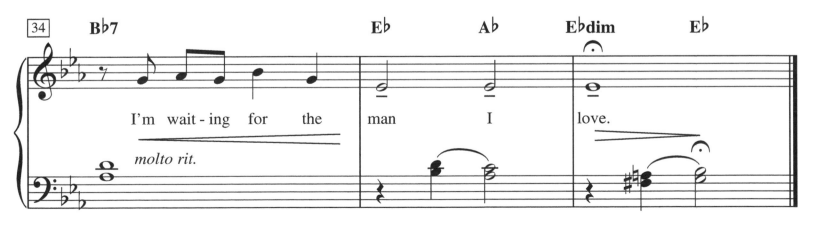

MY ONE AND ONLY

Music and Lyrics by GEORGE GERSHWIN
and IRA GERSHWIN
Arranged by Phillip Keveren

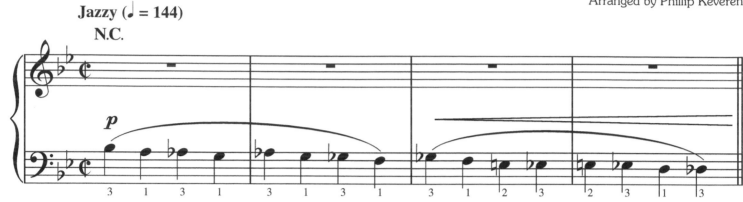

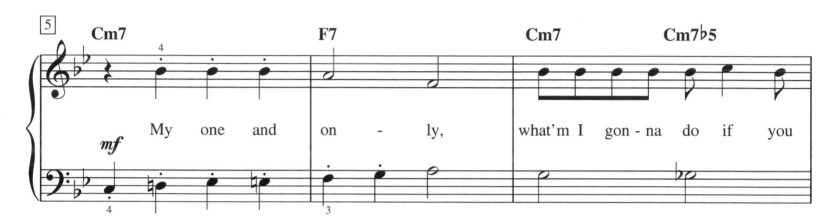

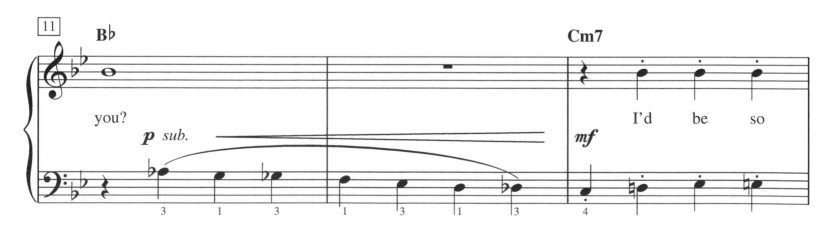

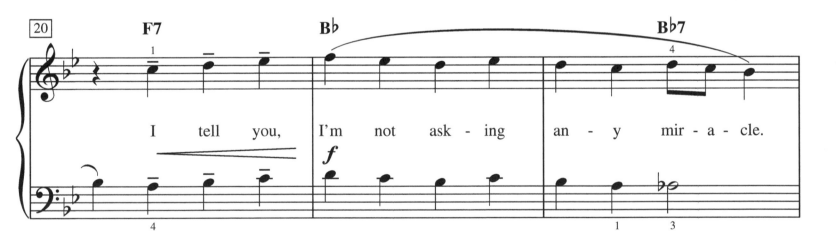

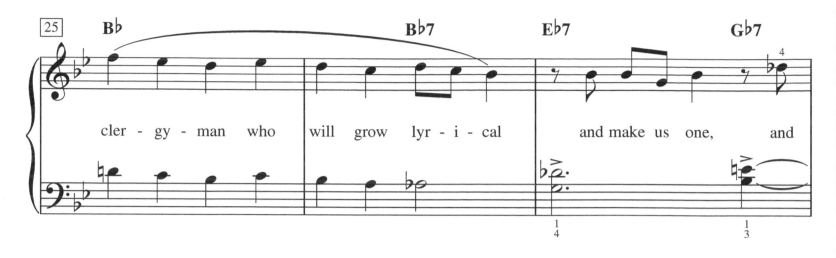

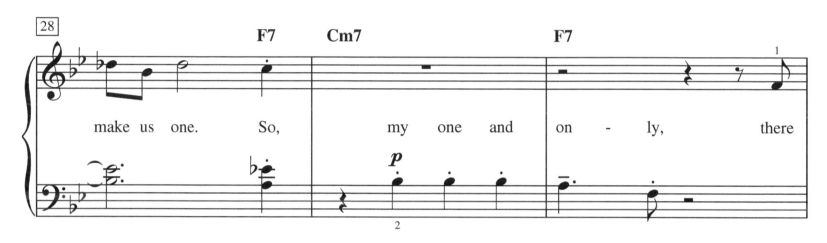

NICE WORK IF YOU CAN GET IT

from A DAMSEL IN DISTRESS

Music and Lyrics by GEORGE GERSHWIN
and IRA GERSHWIN
Arranged by Phillip Keveren

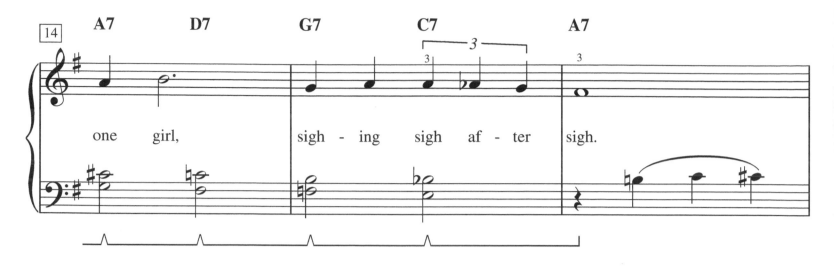

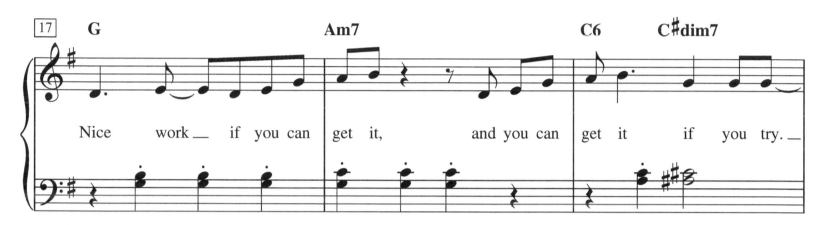

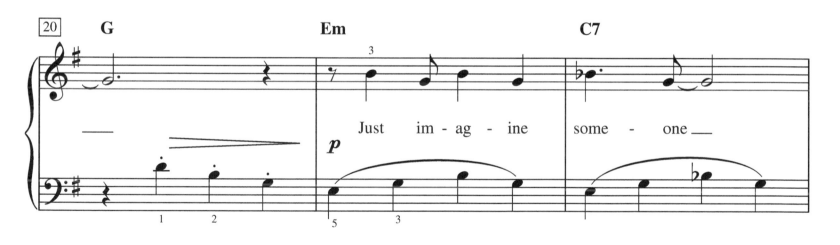

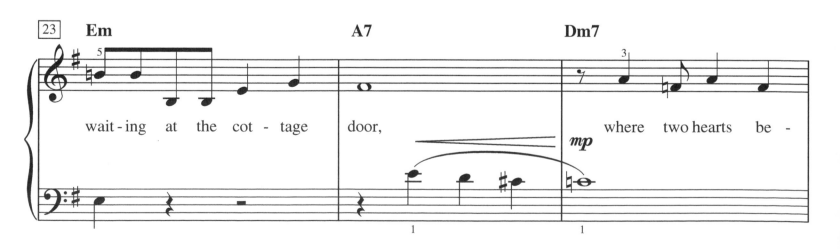

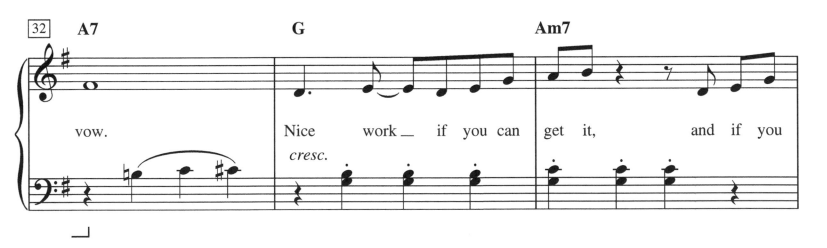

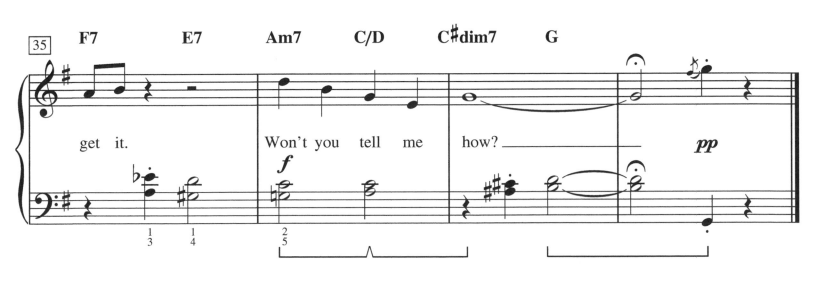

OF THEE I SING

Music and Lyrics by GEORGE GERSHWIN
and IRA GERSHWIN
Arranged by Phillip Keveren

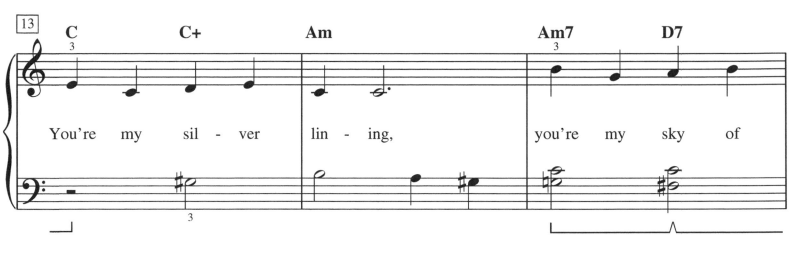

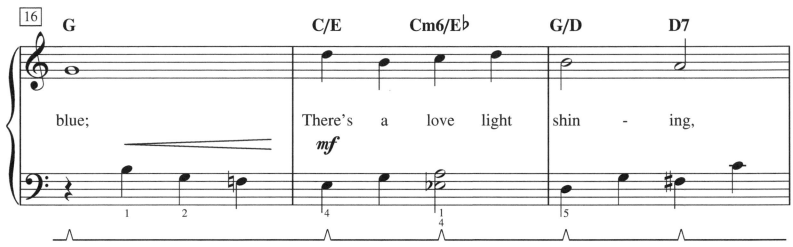

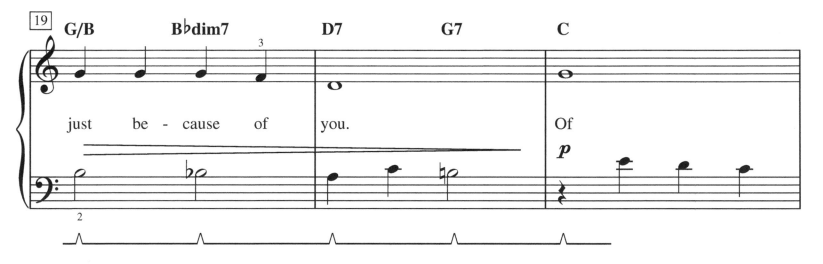

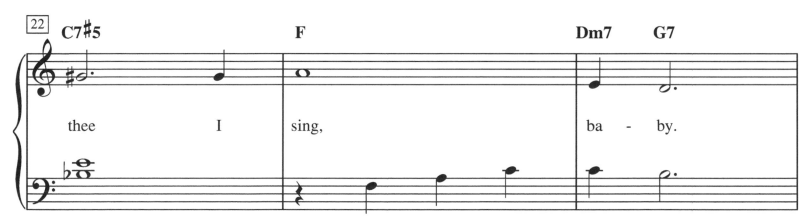

'S WONDERFUL

from FUNNY FACE
from AN AMERICAN IN PARIS

Music and Lyrics by GEORGE GERSHWIN
and IRA GERSHWIN
Arranged by Phillip Keveren

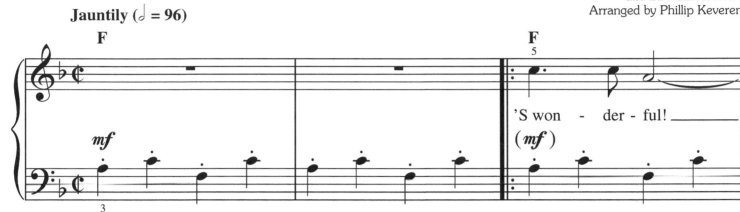

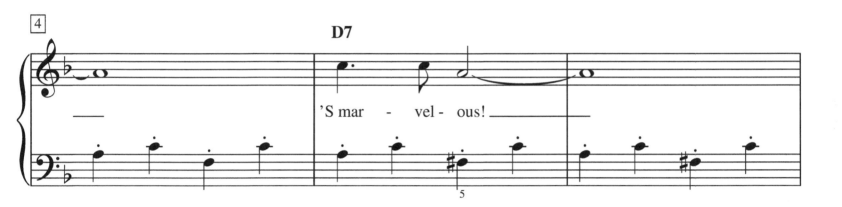

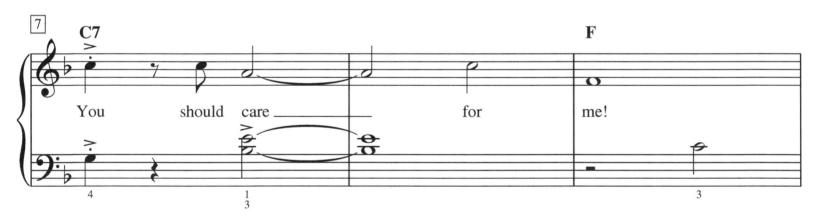

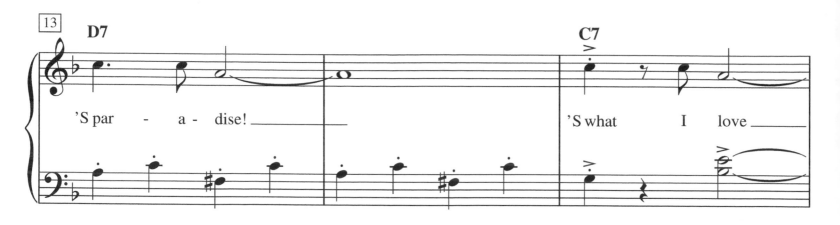

13 **D7** / **C7**

'S par - a - dise! _____ 'S what I love _____

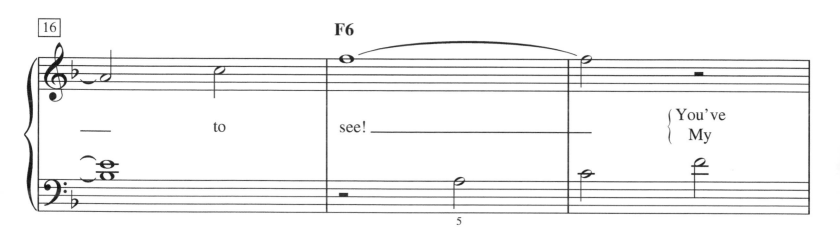

16 / **F6**

___ to see! _____ You've / My

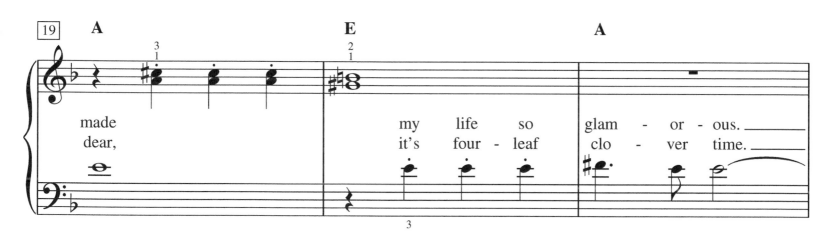

19 **A** / **E** / **A**

made dear, my life so glam - or - ous. ___
it's four - leaf clo - ver time. ___

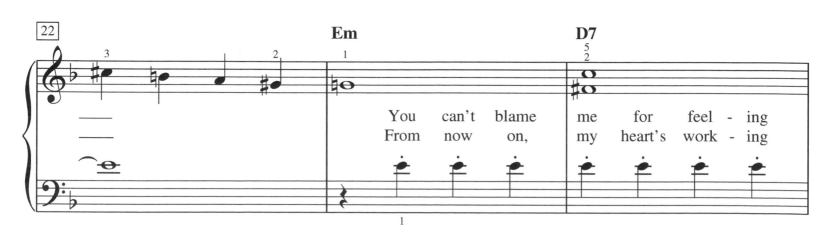

22 / **Em** / **D7**

___ You can't blame me for feel - ing
___ From now on, my heart's work - ing

OH, LADY BE GOOD!

Music and Lyrics by GEORGE GERSHWIN
and IRA GERSHWIN
Arranged by Phillip Keveren

SOMEONE TO WATCH OVER ME

from OH, KAY!

Music and Lyrics by GEORGE GERSHWIN
and IRA GERSHWIN
Arranged by Phillip Keveren

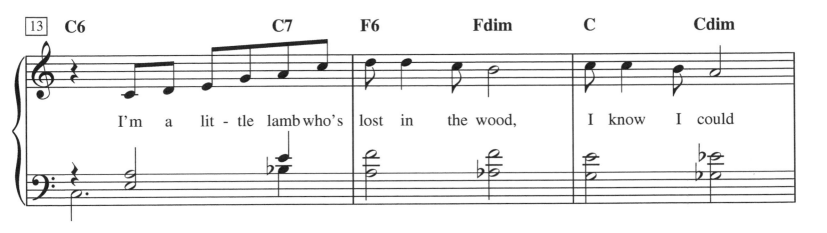

I'm a lit - tle lamb who's lost in the wood, I know I could

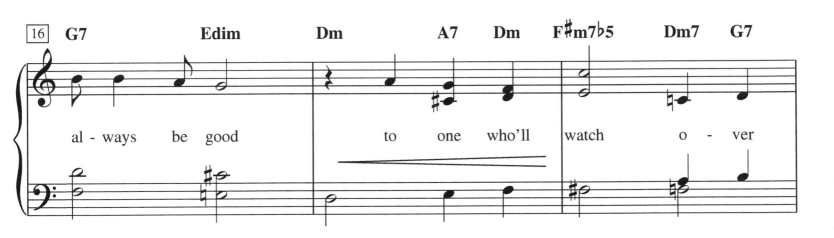

al - ways be good to one who'll watch o - ver

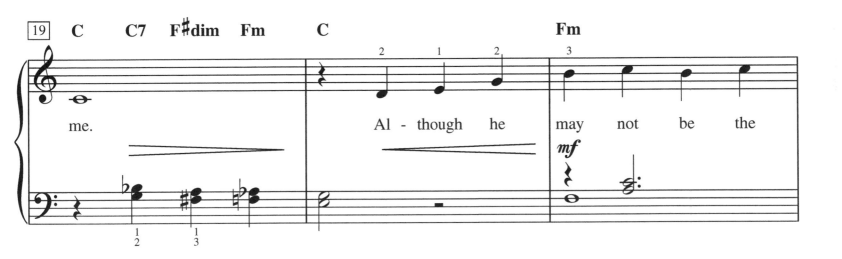

me. Al - though he may not be the

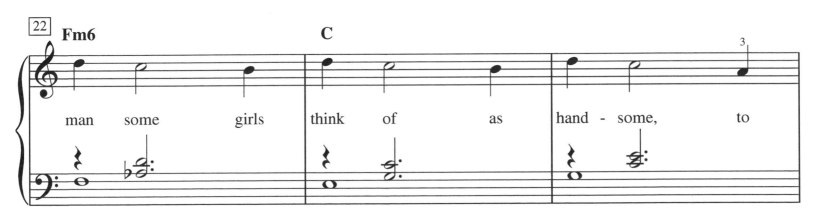

man some girls think of as hand - some, to

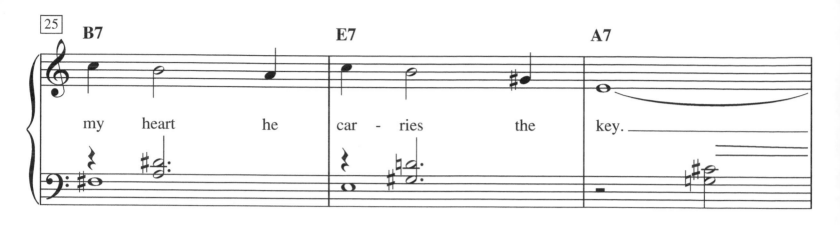

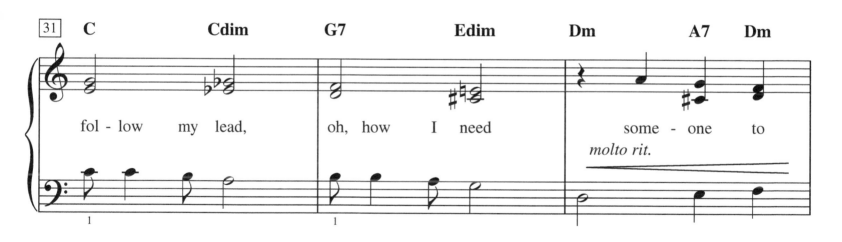

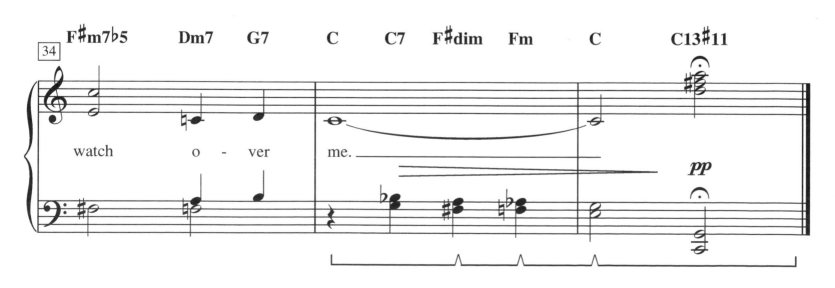

STRIKE UP THE BAND

from STRIKE UP THE BAND

Music and Lyrics by GEORGE GERSHWIN
and IRA GERSHWIN
Arranged by Phillip Keveren

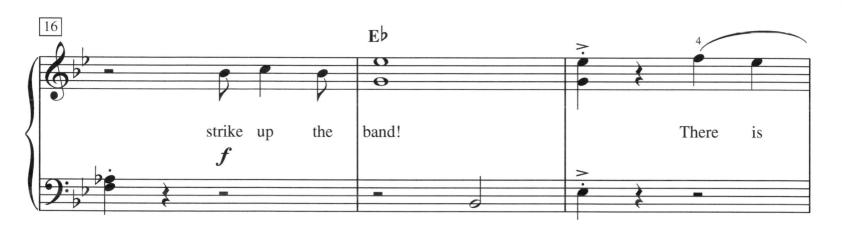

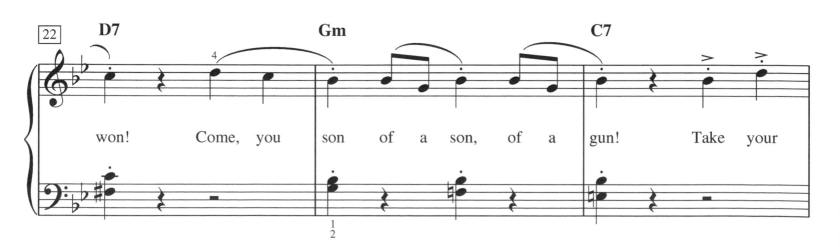

THEY CAN'T TAKE THAT AWAY FROM ME

from THE BARKLEYS OF BROADWAY
from SHALL WE DANCE

Music and Lyrics by GEORGE GERSHWIN
and IRA GERSHWIN
Arranged by Phillip Keveren

THE PHILLIP KEVEREN SERIES

PIANO SOLO

Prices, contents, and availability subject to change without notice.

0422
158

HAL•LEONARD®

Search songlists, more products and place your order from your favorite music retailer at **halleonard.com**

Disney characters and artwork
TM & © 2021 Disney LLC